DINOSAUR PROFILES

IGUANODON

Titles in the Dinosaur Profiles series include:

DINOSAUR PROFILES

IGUANODON

Text by Fabio Marco Dalla Vecchia
Illustrations by Leonello Calvetti and Luca Massini

BLACKBIRCH PRESS
An imprint of Thomson Gale, a part of The Thomson Corporation

Detroit •

For more information, contact
The Gale Group, Inc.
27500 Drake Rd.
Farmington Hills, MI 48331-3535
Or you can visit our Internet site at http://www.gale.com

Computer illustrations 3D and 2D: Leonello Calvetti and Luca Massini

Photographs: pages 20-21, Fabio Marco Dalla Vecchia

LIBRARY OF CONGRESS CATALOGING-IN-PUBLICATION DATA

Dalla Vecchia, Fabio Marco.
Iguanodon / text by Fabio Marco Dalla Vecchia ; illustrations by Leonello Calvetti and Luca Massini.
    p. cm.—(Dinosaur profiles)
Includes bibliographical references and index.
ISBN-13: 978-1-4103-0736-1 (hardcover)
ISBN-10: 1-4103-0736-0 (hardcover)
1. Iguanodon—Juvenile literature. I. Calvetti, Leonello, ill. II. Massini, Luca, ill.
III. Title.

QE862.O65D36 2007
567.914—dc22
                                                                    2006101548

Printed in the United States of America
10 9 8 7 6 5 4 3 2 1

CONTENTS

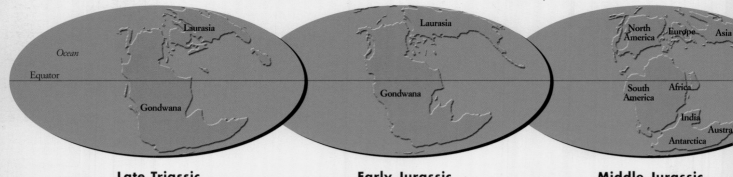

Late Triassic
228–206 million years ago

Early Jurassic
206–176 million years ago

Middle Jurassic
176–161 million years ago

A Changing World

Earth's long history began 4.6 billion years ago. Dinosaurs are some of the most fascinating animals from the planet's long past.

The word *dinosaur* comes from the word *dinosauria*. This word was invented by the English scientist Richard Owen in 1842. It comes from two Greek words, *deinos* and *sauros*. Together, these words mean "terrifying lizards."

The dinosaur era, also called the Mesozoic era, lasted from 228 million years ago to 65 million years ago. It is divided into three periods. The first, the Triassic period, lasted about 42 million years. The second, the Jurassic period, lasted 61 million years. The third, the Cretaceous period, lasted about 79 million years. Dinosaurs ruled the world for a huge time span of 160 million years.

Like dinosaurs, mammals appeared at the end of the Triassic period. During the time of dinosaurs, mammals were small animals the size of a mouse. Only after dinosaurs became extinct did mammals develop

Late Jurassic
1–144 million years ago

Early Cretaceous
144–100 million years ago

Late Cretaceous
100–65 million years ago

into the many forms that exist today. Humans never met Mesozoic dinosaurs. The dinosaurs were gone nearly 65 million years before humans appeared on Earth.

Dinosaurs changed in time. Stegosaurus and Brachiosaurus no longer existed when Tyrannosaurus and Triceratops appeared 75 million years later.

The dinosaur world was different from today's world. The climate was warmer, with few extremes. The position of the continents was different. Plants were constantly changing, and grass did not even exist.

A Gentle Plant Eater

Iguanodon is one of the best-known dinosaurs and has been studied more than any other. The name *Iguanodon* comes from the Greek. It means "iguana tooth." The man who discovered these dinosaurs gave them this name. He thought their teeth looked just like those of iguana lizards, only much bigger.

There were several species of Iguanodon. The adults of the largest species were up to 36 feet (11m) long and weighed around 4 to 5 tons (3.6 to 4.5 metric tons). Despite its huge size, this dinosaur, like all Iguanodons, was a gentle plant eater. Another species of Iguanodon was much smaller. It was only 16 to 23 feet (5 to 7 m) long. Both species lived in the same places and at the same times. Some paleontologists (scientists who study dinosaurs) think the two were actually the same species. They believe the larger ones were the males and the smaller ones were the females.

An adult Iguanodon usually moved on four feet. But if it had to run, it could do so using only its two back legs.

Iguanodon belongs to the order ornithischia. It lived on Earth for most of the early Cretaceous period, from 144 to 100 million years ago. Most Iguanodons lived in what is now Europe, but some have been discovered in Mongolia and in North America.

NORTH
AMERICA

LAURASIA

England

Germany

France

Spain

Tropic of Cancer

TETHYS
OCEAN

AFRICA

This map shows Europe during
the early Cretaceous period.
The red dots show where
Iguanodon fossils have been
discovered.

Iguanodon Babies

Baby Iguanodons looked a lot like adults. But they had larger heads compared to their bodies. They also had much shorter snouts than adults, and enormous eyes. Their arms were much shorter than their legs. This might mean that, unlike their parents, they mainly moved around on their back legs. This would have helped them get away from predators faster than they could have on four legs.

Dangerous Places

Because many Iguanodon fossils have been found together, scientists think the animals lived in herds. Iguanodons lived along the edges of swamps and marshes. In these places, crocodiles and quicksand were dangers. Iguanodons had a spiky thumb on each hand. They may have used these spikes to defend themselves against predators.

PLANT FOODS

Iguanodons were probably able to find plenty of food. Smaller dinosaurs could eat only leaves and branches at the base of trees. But Iguanodon could stand on its back legs to reach the higher branches.

Each Iguanodon had a small, toothless beak like a bird's at the end of its snout. An Iguanodon used this beak to tear off food, which it then chewed in its jaws. Cheek pouches kept the food from sliding outside the mouth as the Iguanodon chewed.

UNDER ATTACK

Several kinds of meat-eating dinosaurs preyed on Iguanodon. The sharp-toothed Neovenator was a fearsome predator. It ranged from 23 to 33 feet (7 to 10 m) long.

Another predator was the smaller Eotyrannus, a relative of Tyrannosaurus. This animal was only about 13 to 16 feet (4 to 5 m) long. The largest and strongest predator of all was Baryonyx. It could grow to be nearly 40 feet (12m) long, and it had an enormous claw on its front foot. Luckily for Iguanodon, this dinosaur most likely preferred to eat fish when it could.

THE IGUANODON BODY

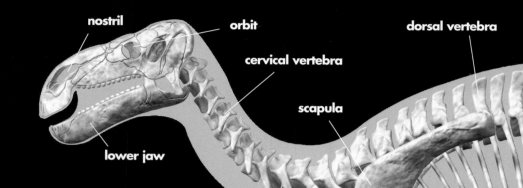

nostril

orbit

dorsal vertebra

cervical vertebra

scapula

lower jaw

front foot

The Iguanodon skull was long and shaped a little like a horse's. The largest species of Iguanodon had 29 rows of teeth in the upper jaw and 25 rows of teeth in the lower jaw. The teeth were leaf-shaped, with ridges. Because this dinosaur ate tough plant foods, its teeth gradually wore away. But when a tooth wore down, a new one grew in to take its place.

Iguanodon's front arms had five-fingered hands. One of these fingers was a cone-shaped spike. The spike might have been used for defense or to split fruits and seeds. The smaller species of Iguanodon had bigger spikes than the larger species did.

The back legs were much longer, larger, and stronger than the front legs. The back feet had three toes. Meat-eating dinosaurs had sharp claws, but Iguanodons had flat, rounded nails.

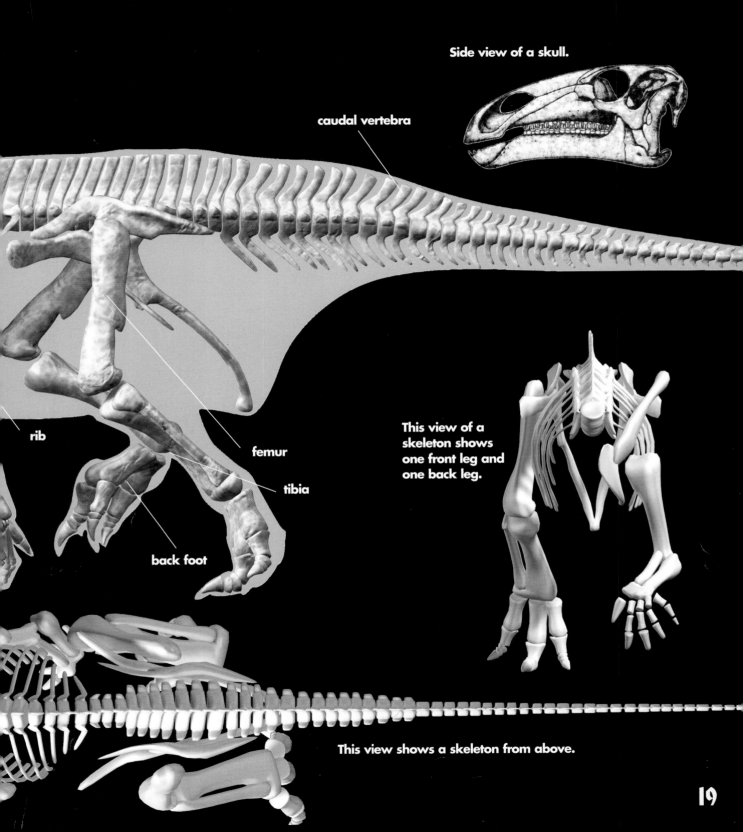

Side view of a skull.

caudal vertebra

rib

femur

tibia

back foot

This view of a skeleton shows one front leg and one back leg.

This view shows a skeleton from above.

19

Digging Up Iguanodon

The first Iguanodon remains found were a few teeth. In 1822, Mary Mantell discovered the teeth in a pile of gravel by the side of a road in England. She gave them to her husband, Dr. Gideon Mantell. In 1825, Dr. Mantell published a description of these fossils, saying that they came from a large plant-eating reptile. In this paper, he called the creature Iguanodon.

The gravel where the teeth were found had come from a quarry in southern England. In 1834, workers at the quarry gave Dr. Mantell other parts of an Iguanodon skeleton. When he tried to figure out what the dinosaur looked like, Dr. Mantell made some mistakes. He thought the spiky thumb was a horn that was located at the end of the snout. He also thought Iguanodon teeth looked like those of an iguana lizard. So he believed Iguanodon must have looked like a giant iguana, with four legs all the same length.

In 1851, workers used these ideas when they built life-size models of Iguanodon for a fair in London. The models looked like huge rhinoceroses with scales!

Later, in 1878, workers in a coal mine in Belgium discovered many complete Iguanodon skeletons. These fossils helped scientists understand what the creatures really looked like. Today, some of those fossils are on display at the Royal Belgian Institute of Natural Sciences in Brussels, Belgium.

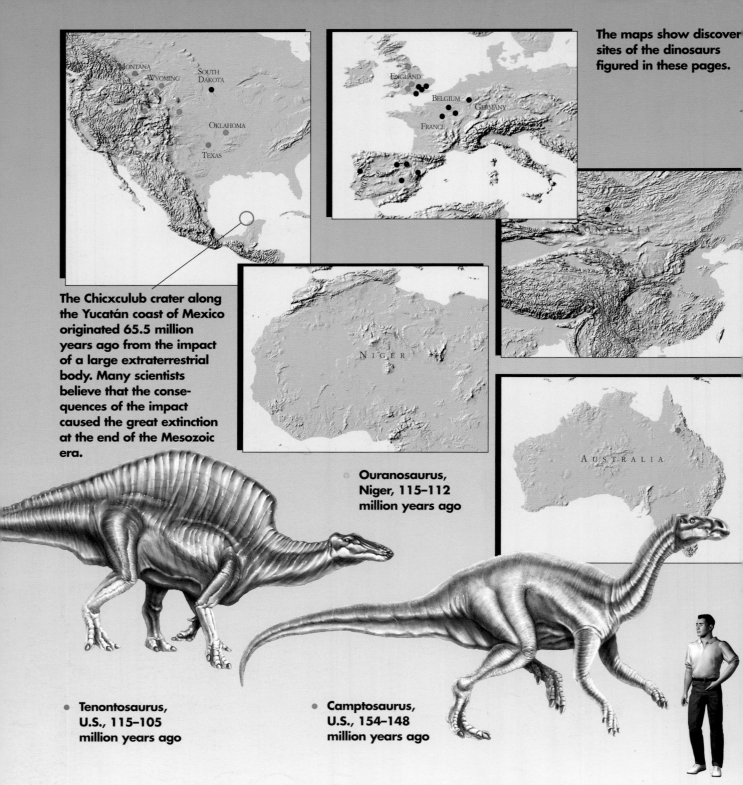

The maps show discover
sites of the dinosaurs
figured in these pages.

The Chicxculub crater along
the Yucatán coast of Mexico
originated 65.5 million
years ago from the impact
of a large extraterrestrial
body. Many scientists
believe that the conse-
quences of the impact
caused the great extinction
at the end of the Mesozoic
era.

Ouranosaurus,
Niger, 115–112
million years ago

Tenontosaurus,
U.S., 115–105
million years ago

Camptosaurus,
U.S., 154–148
million years ago

THE IGUANODONTS

The Iguanodonts and their relatives spread throughout the world. Around the middle of the Cretaceous period, they gave rise to the hadrosaurids, or duck-billed dinosaurs.

Altirhinus, Mongolia, 125–100 million years ago

Muttaburrasaurus, Australia, 110–100 million years ago

Iguanodon, England, Belgium, Spain, Portugal, France, Germany, Mongolia, U.S. 140–100 million years ago

THE GREAT EXTINCTION

Sixty-five million years ago, 70 million years after the time of Iguanodon, dinosaurs became extinct. This may have happened because a large meteorite struck Earth. A wide crater caused by a meteorite 65 million years ago has been located along the coast of the Yucatán Peninsula in Mexico. The impact of the meteorite would have produced an enormous amount of dust. This dust would have stayed suspended in the atmosphere and blocked sunlight for a long time. A lack of sunlight would have caused a drastic drop in the earth's temperature and killed plants. The plant-eating dinosaurs would have died, starved and frozen. As a result, meat-eating dinosaurs would have had no prey and would also have starved.

Some scientists believe dinosaurs did not die out completely. They think that birds were feathered dinosaurs that survived the great extinction. That would make the present-day chicken and all of its feathered relatives descendants of the large dinosaurs.

THE EVOLUTION OF DINOSAURS

The oldest dinosaur fossils are 220–225 million years old and have been found mainly in South America. They have also been found in Africa, India, and North America. Dinosaurs probably evolved from small and nimble bipedal reptiles like the Triassic Lagosuchus of Argentina. Dinosaurs were able to rule the world because their legs were held directly under the body, like those of modern mammals. This made them faster and less clumsy than other reptiles.

Since 1887, dinosaurs have been divided into two groups based on the structure of their hips. Saurischian dinosaurs had hips shaped like those of modern lizards. Ornithischian dinosaurs had hips shaped like those of modern birds.

Triceratops is one of the ornithischian dinosaurs, whose hip bones (inset) are shaped like those of modern birds.

There are two main groups of saurischians. One group is the sauropodomorphs. This group includes sauropods, such as Brachiosaurus. Sauropods ate plants and were quadrupedal, meaning they walked on four legs. The other group of saurischians, theropods, includes bipedal meat-eating predators. Some paleontologists believe birds are a branch of theropod dinosaurs.

Ornithischians are all plant eaters. They are divided into three groups. Thyreophorans include the quadrupedal stegosaurians, including Stegosaurus, and ankylosaurians, including Ankylosaurus. The other two groups are ornithopods, which includes Edmontosaurus, and marginocephalians.

A Dinosaur's Family Tree

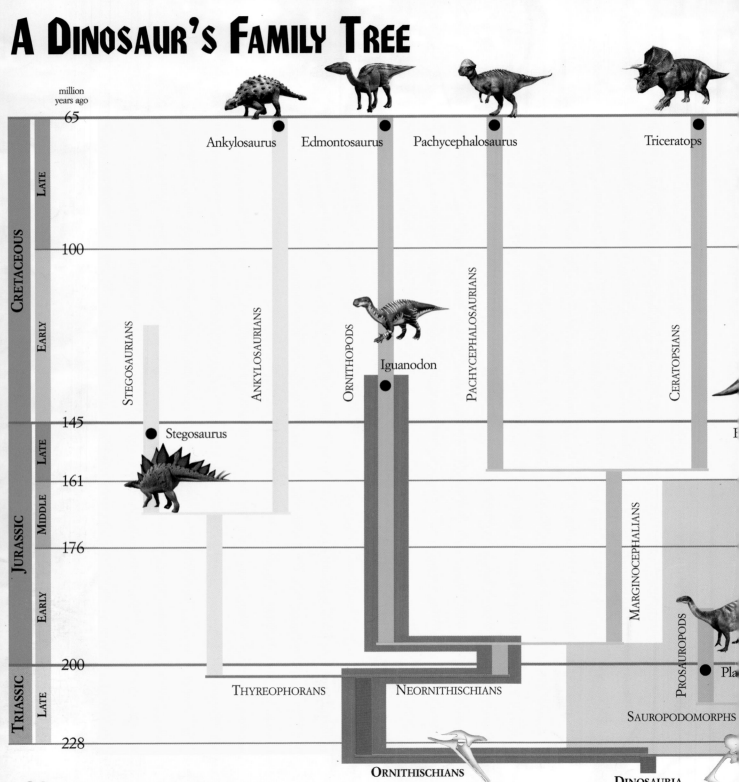

million years ago

65

CRETACEOUS

LATE

100

EARLY

145

JURASSIC

LATE

161

MIDDLE

176

EARLY

200

TRIASSIC

LATE

228

Ankylosaurus

Edmontosaurus

Pachycephalosaurus

Triceratops

STEGOSAURIANS

ANKYLOSAURIANS

ORNITHOPODS

Iguanodon

PACHYCEPHALOSAURIANS

CERATOPSIANS

Stegosaurus

MARGINOCEPHALIANS

PROSAUROPODS

Pla

THYREOPHORANS

NEORNITHISCHIANS

SAUROPODOMORPHS

ORNITHISCHIANS

DINOSAURIA

26

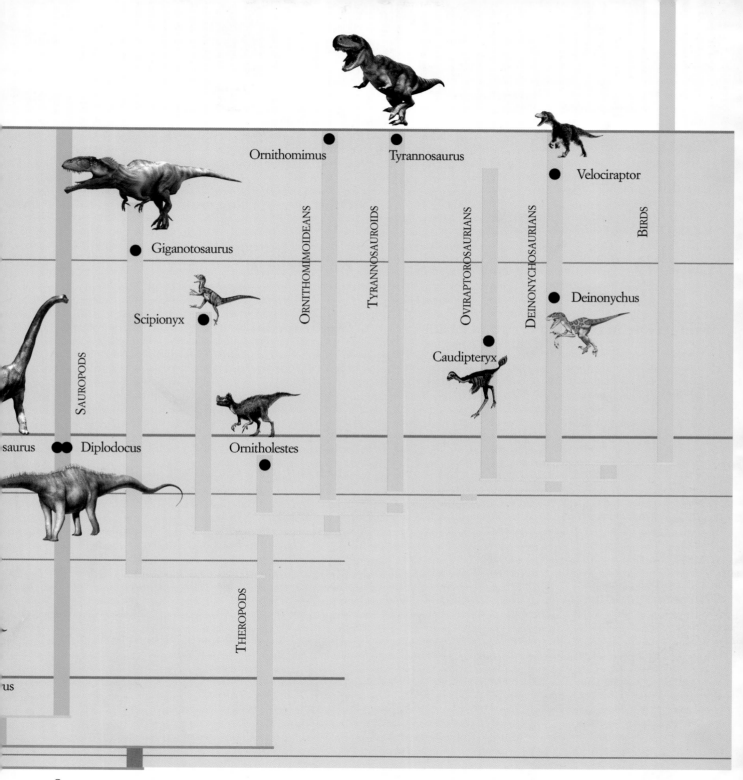

Ornithomimus

Tyrannosaurus

Velociraptor

ORNITHOMIMOIDEANS

TYRANNOSAUROIDS

OVIRAPTOROSAURIANS

DEINONYCHOSAURIANS

Giganotosaurus

Deinonychus

Scipionyx

Caudipteryx

SAUROPODS

Diplodocus

...saurus

Ornitholestes

THEROPODS

...us

SAURISCHIANS

Glossary

Bipedal moving on two feet

Caudal related to the tail

Cervical related to the neck

Claws sharp, pointed nails on the fingers and toes of predators

Cretaceous period the period of geological time between 144 and 65 million years ago

Dorsal related to the back

Evolution changes in living things over time

Femur thigh bone

Fossil part of a living thing, such as a skeleton or leaf imprint, that has been preserved in Earth's crust from an earlier geological age

Jurassic period the period of geological time between 206 and 144 million years ago

Mesozoic era the period of geological time between 248 and 65 million years ago

Meteorite a piece of iron or rock that falls to Earth from space

Orbit the opening in the skull surrounding the eye

Paleontologist a scientist who studies prehistoric life

Quadrupedal moving on four feet

Quarry a place where stone is removed from the earth

Scapula shoulder blade

Skeleton the structure of an animal body, made up of bones

Skull the bones that form the head and face

Tibia shinbone

Triassic period the period of geological time between 248 and 206 million years ago

Vertebra a bone of the spine

FOR MORE INFORMATION

Books

Daniel Cohen, *Iguanodon*. Mankato, MN: Bridgestone Books, 2003.

Steve Parker, *1000 Things You Should Know About Dinosaurs*. Broomall, PA: Mason Crest, 2003.

Virginia Schomp, *Iguanodons and Other Spiky-Thumbed Plant Eaters*. New York: Marshall Cavendish Benchmark, 2005.

Web Sites

Dinosaur Guide
http://dsc.discovery.com/guides/dinosaur/dinosaur.html
This Discovery Channel site features a richly illustrated Dinosaur Gallery that includes Iguanodon.

Prehistoric Life
http://www.bbc.co.uk/sn/prehistoric_life/
This section of the BBC Web site contains a great deal of information about dinosaurs, including galleries of illustrations along with games and quizzes.

The Smithsonian National Museum of Natural History
http://www.nmnh.si.edu/paleo/dino/
A virtual tour of the Smithsonian's National Museum of Natural History dinosaur exhibits.

About the Author

Fabio Marco Dalla Vecchia is the curator of the Paleontological Museum of Monfalcone in Gorizia, Italy. He has participated in several paleontological field works in Italy and other countries and has directed paleontological excavations in Italy. He is the author of more than 50 scientific articles that have been published in national and international journals.

INDEX

INDEX